SHIP
MODELS
and how to build them

SHIP
MODELS
and how to build them

BY HARVEY WEISS

Thomas Y. Crowell Company   New York

Copyright © 1973 by Harvey Weiss

Manufactured in the United States of America

1   2   3   4   5   6   7   8   9   10

Library of Congress Cataloging in Publication Data

Weiss, Harvey.
  Ship models and how to build them.

  SUMMARY: Directions for using simple construction methods and tools to make models of a tugboat, sailboat, stern-wheeler, submarine, and other types of boats.

  1. Ship models—Juvenile literature. [1. Ship models] I. Title.
VM298.W37   745,59'28   72-7562
ISBN 0-690-73270-8

CONTENTS

SHIP MODELS

and how to build them

INTRODUCTION

The ship models described in this book are designed so that they can be put together without a lot of fancy, hard-to-find power tools. The construction is simplified. The models are not intended to be precise, museum-quality reproductions, perfect in every detail, enclosed in glass cabinets. Very few people have the interest, time, or patience to spend weeks and months laboring over accurately scaled models of this sort.

The book shows how to make a few basic hull shapes. And these shapes can be used in a variety of ways. In effect, you can design your models to suit your own ideas and preferences. For example, the first chapter gives the plans for a tugboat. But the hull of a tugboat is similar to that of a fireboat, a fishing boat, and a certain kind of sailboat. You can modify the tug, altering the superstructure, the color scheme, and the details, and get the kind of model you want.

The drawings and photographs show the proper or normal way (the author's way) of building the models described. But you may have other ideas. You might want a sailboat with two masts instead of one, or a hull that is narrower than the one shown, or broader and more buoyant—or whatever. By all means change the model to suit your own ideas. If, however, you want your model to travel by sail or power through the water, you will have to give some careful thought to the changes you make, because there are some very specific considerations in the design of floating shapes. For example, if the Mississippi River stern-wheeler is top-heavy it will capsize. If the PT boat has too much weight up forward, it will float with the stern higher than the bow.

Most of these considerations are common sense, and if you are making changes, you can tell by trial and error, by some experimental testing in a bathtub, whether your modifications are workable and practical.

Until recently boat designers—or naval architects, as they are called—started to design a boat not with pencil and paper but with a block of wood and a penknife. The hull was carefully whittled out of the wood. Then it was studied, changed, and refined until the shapes and forms seemed just right. This model was then used as the basis for the full-sized boat. All measurements were taken from the model. Even today naval architects will often make a model before completing full-scale drawings for a new boat. Sometimes the models are used in test tanks. The model is attached to a measurement device, then towed along a very long, water-filled trough. The designers can tell just how a boat will perform at different speeds and under different conditions.

As you work on your models, it is worth keeping in mind that you are building—and designing—not real boats, but *model* boats. Never mind that your model of the H.M.S. *Bounty* may have only two masts, whereas the original had three. If your model has the mood and character you want (or sails well), you've succeeded very well indeed.

THE TOOLS

The tools listed below are all fairly common and most will be found in the average household. However, it is quite certain that at some point you will find you don't have one vital tool or another. And this is when you must use your ingenuity and a little imagination. For example, suppose you didn't have a vise to hold down a piece of wood you were working on. Then you would have to figure out a substitute way of keeping the wood in place. Perhaps you could find a C-clamp. Maybe you could nail the wood to your workbench. Perhaps you could wedge it somewhere.

So don't worry if you don't have all the tools listed here. (After all, look at the elaborate structures beavers make, using only their teeth!) When I was a very young fellow and working on a little ship model, I didn't have a drill, and I remember that my solution was to hold a thin nail with a pair of pliers over the flame of one of the burners on the kitchen stove. When the nail got red-hot, I would *burn* a hole where one was needed. This was slow and primitive, but I had no other way to make a hole—and it did work.

Crosscut Saw

The most generally useful saw is a crosscut saw. This will cut *across* the grain of the wood. (A ripsaw cuts with the grain.) If your crosscut saw is sharp, it will cut fast and easily, and can be used for a lot of the preliminary rough shaping of your models.

3

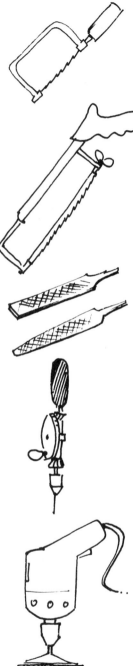

Coping Saw

This saw is used for delicate work and for curved cuts. It is also essential if you are going to cut out an inside section of a plank of wood. To do this, first drill a hole in the wood. Then remove the blade from the saw, pass it through the hole, and reattach it.

Hacksaw

Primarily intended for cutting metal, this saw will also come in handy from time to time for cutting small pieces of wood as well as metal.

Rasps and Files

These are used for roughing out and smoothing wood. A rasp is coarser than a file. You can just about completely shape the form of a boat hull with a big rough rasp. It is a very useful tool.

Hand Drill

A useful tool in a number of ways. You will need a variety of bits to go with it. Useful bit sizes are $1/16$, $1/8$, $3/16$, and $1/4$ inches.

Electric Drill

This is not an essential tool. You can manage without it. But if you can get the use of an electric drill with a sanding disk, you will be able to save yourself a lot of filing and sanding by hand. A rough sandpaper disk on an electric drill will shape and smooth a model hull in remarkably short time.

4

Hammer and Nails

You are no doubt familiar with these tools. Be sure to use the right size of nail. Too big a nail will often split a small piece of wood. Too thin or too short a nail may not hold well. So choose your nails with care. Don't take any chances if you suspect a nail is going to split a piece of wood. Drill a hole where the nail is going to go. The hole should be slightly smaller than the width of the nail. For model making the most useful kind of nail is the brad, or finishing nail, which has a very small head. (Use a small hammer on small nails.)

Sandpaper

This may not seem like a tool at first, but it shapes and smooths wood, so we may as well consider it one. And it is very important. Sandpaper is needed to get the final, smooth, sleek curves that give a model its elegant good looks.

When you use sandpaper, it is important to have a "back-up" block. This is simply a block of wood around which the sandpaper can be wrapped. With a back-up block the sandpaper bears down evenly on the surface you are working on. If you hold the sandpaper in your hand, the bumps are liable to stay bumpy, and the valleys low—which is just what you want to avoid. The only time you don't use a back-up block is when you are sanding some of the inside curves in odd places on a hull.

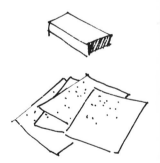

Sandpaper comes in coarse, medium, fine, and extra-fine grades. You'll want a few sheets of each. After your hull is cut and filed to shape, you use the coarse sandpaper to remove all lumps, bumps, and irregularities. Then switch to medium, then fine grades until the wood is as even and smooth as you can get it.

There are various kinds of sandpaper. The inexpensive kind, which uses particles of sand, is worthless. Don't buy it. The kind you want is called "production" paper and uses aluminum oxide particles. This sandpaper will last for an amazingly long time, and is much cheaper in the long run.

When you are sanding small parts, it is best to lay the sandpaper down on a flat surface, and then rub the wood against the paper. You should also try to collect and save the dust you get from sanding and filing. This dust can be mixed with glue to make a paste for filling small holes and cracks in wood.

Knife

Everybody has a pocket- or jackknife—often a sturdy one of good quality. But very few people have a really *sharp* knife. For modelmaking your knife must be just as sharp as you can make it, or it will do more damage than good.

Chisels and Gouges

A chisel has a straight edge; a gouge has a rounded or U-shaped edge. The gouge is particularly useful when you are working on curves that go inward. Both tools are useless unless sharp.

Plane

This is really a straight-edge chisel. But the cutting edge is held in a metal frame that permits it to dig into the wood only a fraction of an inch. As a result, the plane cuts a thin flat ribbon of wood as it is pushed along.

Sharpening Stone

There is no point in trying to use a knife, chisel, gouge, or plane unless you have a carborundum sharpening stone to keep them sharp. The cutting edge of these tools is sharpened by holding it firmly in two hands and rubbing it carefully back and forth on the stone. These stones usually have a coarse grain on one side and a fine grain on the other. Use a little household oil as a lubricant as you work. When you sharpen any cutting tool on a sharpening stone, be careful to keep the beveled edge always at the same angle. This will give you an even, straight bevel. If you keep changing the angle, or rock the tool back and forth, you will get a rounded bevel, as shown in the margin, and this will not cut well.

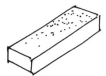

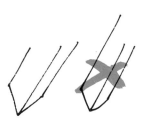

Vise

This is a holding tool. Without it much of the cutting, filing, and sanding you do will be awkward and uncomfortable. The bigger the vise the better, and it should be attached to a solid, heavy worktable. When you put a fragile part of your model in the vise, be careful that the pressure of the jaws doesn't scar or scratch it. Wrap the jaws with tape, or use thin strips of wood as a cushion. There is only one really efficient way to hold a ship model in a vise when you are shaping the hull, and that is to attach a block of wood to the deck of the hull by means of screws or nails, then clamp the block in your vise. When the hull is completed, the block can be removed, and the nail or screw holes filled—or most likely covered over with hatches or cabins or whatever structure attaches to the deck.

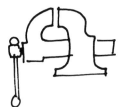

Light

It may seem obvious that you need good light to see what you are doing. But many people just don't give this matter any thought. Try to set up your work area near a window, or get a good lamp or two and place it where it will shine on your work—and not in your eyes.

THE MATERIALS

Wood

The basic material for the models described in this book is clear pine. It is available in any lumberyard. It comes in a variety of sizes, such as 1 inch × 1 inch, 1 inch × 6 inches, ½ inch × 2 inches, and so on, in any length from a foot up to sixteen feet. The larger and heavier wood sizes such as 2 × 4 or 4 × 4 inches, however, are not usually available in clear pine, and you may have to settle for something similar. If you explain what you want the wood for, the lumberyard will usually be able to suggest a practical alternative.

There are many other kinds of wood which you can use as well as clear pine, of course. Beautiful models have been made from old orange-crate lumber, or miscellaneous scraps found in junk piles. Sometimes what looks like a dirty, useless piece of wood will turn out to be perfectly good once the outside layer is planed or sanded off.

What you must avoid, however, is wood that is split or warped. Knotholes are also a source of trouble. They are almost impossible to whittle or chisel, and are liable to show through and mar a finished surface. Don't ever use plywood. It is difficult to cut, tricky to carve, and hard to finish.

When you buy wood at a lumberyard, it is important to remember that the sizes of wood refer to the unfinished size of the piece. The wood is planed smooth before it is sold, and this process removes about a quarter of an inch from each dimension. If, for example, you buy a piece that is 3 feet long and 2×4 inches, you will find when you measure it that it is actually 3 feet long and $1\frac{3}{4} \times 3\frac{3}{4}$ inches. A piece 1×2 inches will measure about $\frac{3}{4} \times 1\frac{3}{4}$ inches, and so on. So if the size of the wood you are buying is critical, you had best ask at the lumberyard what the actual dimensions are.

Another kind of wood you will need is dowels. These are simply "rods" of hardwood. They come in three-foot lengths and in various diameters, up to an inch. They are extremely useful for masts, smokestacks, and a great many other boat parts. When you buy dowels (you can get them at lumberyards and hardware stores) choose them carefully, avoiding any that are warped or that don't have an even, straight grain.

IMPROVISE. It is very likely that you won't always have exactly the size and kind of materials needed for the models described here. You may not be able to go to a lumberyard. Or the lumberyard may not have just what you want. Or you may be using scrap materials. In such cases you must improvise. If a piece of wood is too large, cut it down to size. If the wood is too small, glue several pieces together. If the plans call for a thin dowel and you don't have one, whittle a twig to size, or use a piece of stiff wire or a strip of plastic or whatever you can lay your hands on that can be made to do the job. There is always an alternative.

Glues

If your models are not going to be put in water, you can use any white, casein glue such as Elmer's. This is a strong, permanent glue. But if the joint you make with this glue is soaked for any length of time, it will loosen and come apart. If your models are going to "go to sea," you need a waterproof glue. These glues usually come in two parts. You mix the parts together in the quantity you need, following the directions on the container. Then you apply the glue, clamp or weight the parts, and wait six or more hours until the glue dries. The container will tell you what the drying time is. This kind of joint will never come apart—even if permanently submerged.

When you glue two pieces of wood together, it is very important that both pieces come into complete contact with one another. Unless the glue forms a layer touching *both* surfaces of the wood, you won't get good adhesion. This means that before the pieces are joined, you must sand or file both surfaces so that they are in complete contact over the entire glued area.

Something else many people don't realize is that when two painted surfaces are glued together, the attachment is of paint layer to paint layer. If the paint peels off the wood easily, the joint will come apart easily—even if you have used the strongest glue in the world.

Paints

A well-made model can be ruined by a sloppy paint job. So don't get impatient and rush to finish with a slapdash coat of whatever paint happens to be handy. The proper way to paint a model is like this:

1. When you have finished your final sanding, brush

away all dust and apply a coat of sealer. This can be shellac or varnish and serves to seal the wood so that the following coats of paint will go on smoothly. If you are fussy and want a really professional-looking, glass-smooth surface, apply a coat of filler before you put on the sealer. (A "filler" is a paint to which some sort of finely ground powder has been added. This powder gets into the tiny cracks and pores of the wood, filling them up.) The filler is brushed on, allowed to dry for about fifteen minutes, after which the excess is wiped off with a rough rag. The wood is allowed to dry overnight and then sanded.

2. When the sealer coat is dry, sand lightly with a fine sandpaper, wipe off the dust, then apply your paint. Don't try to paint with some scruffy old brush with mangled bristles. And use a brush of the proper size. A 1-inch brush is about right for the average model. For details use a small round brush. Clean your brushes with the proper solvent when you are done. The paint-can label will tell you what the proper solvent is for the paint you are using. Turpentine is the solvent for oil-base paints, water for water-base paints, and alcohol is the solvent for shellac. (If you can lay your hands on some of the paints that come in pressurized spray cans, you will get a neater job than with a brush.)

3. After the first coat of paint has dried, sand lightly with extra-fine sandpaper, dust off, then apply your next coat. Most models don't need more than two coats.

There are special paints made for models. They come in small bottles and are available in almost any color. But if you are covering a large area, or using many colors, they become quite expensive. In most cases you can use any good paint, either glossy (shiny) or mat (dull), according to your preference. As a rule, a carefully applied enamel paint will look best.

When you want to get a neat edge on an area of paint, you must use masking tape. This is a sticky paper tape. You press it onto your model, leaving the area to be painted uncovered. Then you paint up to and slightly over the edge of the tape. After the paint has been applied, peel away the tape, and you will have a clean, crisp edge that looks very professional. (You don't have to wait for the paint to dry before removing the masking tape.) Once you get the hang of using masking tape you'll find it indispensable.

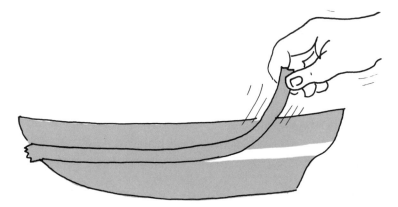

In general it is best to paint as many separate parts of your model as possible before they are assembled. This is especially true when the parts are different colors. You'll get a much neater job this way.

Some people prefer to leave their ship models unpainted. They simply apply a coat of varnish. If the model is neatly made from good wood with a nice grain, and if there aren't too many patched holes and gouges, this kind of unpainted finish can be very attractive.

HOW TO USE THE SCALE DRAWINGS

The plans for the models in this book are drawn on blue-squared backgrounds. If you want to be very accurate and careful, you can transfer these squares onto your wood. Then you can use the squares as guides in copying the actual lines of the model onto the wood.

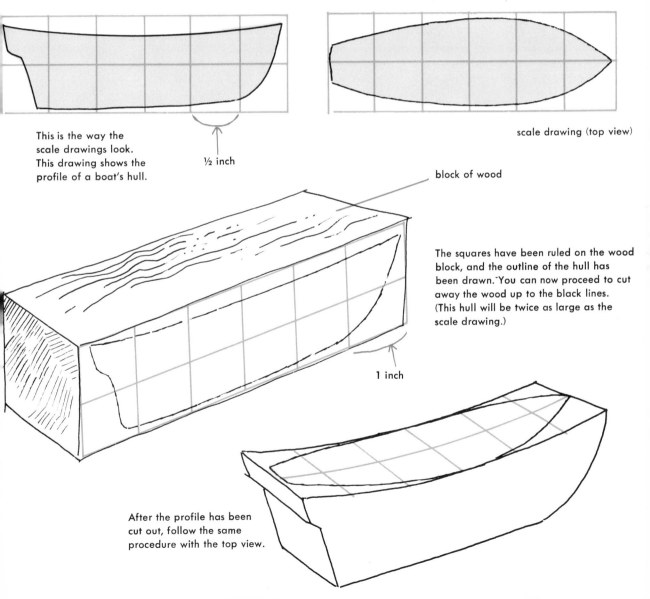

This is the way the scale drawings look. This drawing shows the profile of a boat's hull.

½ inch

scale drawing (top view)

block of wood

The squares have been ruled on the wood block, and the outline of the hull has been drawn. You can now proceed to cut away the wood up to the black lines. (This hull will be twice as large as the scale drawing.)

1 inch

After the profile has been cut out, follow the same procedure with the top view.

Vertical cross sections of the hull are shown as solid blue silhouettes. A cross section is like a slice of salami. It is a vertical slice of the hull. In order to save space, only half the slice is shown. Inasmuch as boat hulls are symmetrical, there is no need to show the entire slice. Whenever a cross section is shown, a notation tells you where the slice has been made. The cross section would be of no use unless you knew just where it belonged on the hull.

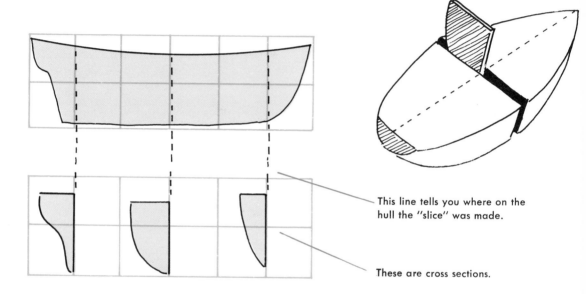

This line tells you where on the hull the "slice" was made.

These are cross sections.

When large, precise models are made, these cross sections are traced onto pieces of cardboard. Then the cardboard inside the outline is cut away. This gives you what is called a "template." The template is placed against the side of the hull. When the hull is cut to the right shape, the template will fit snugly up against it, and you will know that you have carved exactly the correct shape. A plan for a large model may have as many as ten or twelve of these cross sections and templates.

14

This is how a template is made.

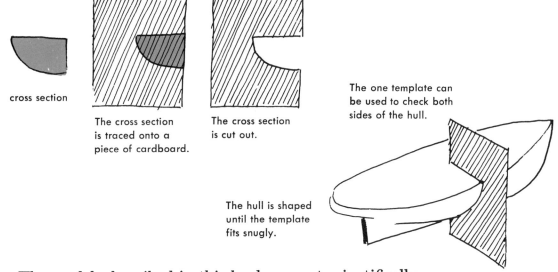

cross section

The cross section is traced onto a piece of cardboard.

The cross section is cut out.

The one template can be used to check both sides of the hull.

The hull is shaped until the template fits snugly.

The models described in this book are not scientifically exact reproductions of any particular boat, so there is no real need for templates or very precise measurements. But you can look at the cross sections and tell just what the shape of the hull should be. The hull of most boats is like a piece of sculpture. It has a smooth, graceful form and a shape that is nice to touch. If the models you make have this feeling, you have accomplished a great deal, and you will have a beautiful object—even if the finished product doesn't turn out to look too much like the original.

The plans in this book are mostly half size. In other words, if each of the blue squares is ½ inch in the book, the actual size on your wood block should be 1 inch square. If you want, you could very well change the scale to suit your own ideas. Perhaps you want a very small or a very large model. You could make the squares on your wood the same size as they are in the book—or you could make them 1½ inches square. (If you made them 1 foot square you might end up with a full-sized boat and could steam off to a South Pacific island!)

1. A TUGBOAT

If you've never made a wooden model, or if you haven't had much experience working with wood, it would be an excellent idea to start with the model described here—even if you really want to make something large and elaborate like a battleship or a three-masted clipper ship. This little tugboat with its solid hull is very easy to make, and the instructions are quite detailed and will introduce you to some of the techniques of modelmaking. (The hull for this tugboat is the same as the one used for the little sailboat described in the second chapter.)

MATERIALS

    One piece of 2- × 4-inch wood (or the equivalent), 9 inches long, for the hull

    One piece of 2- × 2-inch wood (or the equivalent), 5 inches long, for the cabin and wheelhouse

    One ¾-inch piece of dowel (or the equivalent), about 3 inches long, for the smokestack

    Miscellaneous scraps of wood and odds and ends

    1. Cut your wood for the hull to the proper size. Instead of using a 2- × 4-inch piece for the hull you could glue together two pieces of 1- × 4-inch wood. This might even be preferable because 2 × 4's are a size used for construction and building, and most often the wood is spruce. Sizes such as 1 × 4, on the other hand, are usually pine, which is a more even-grained wood and better for modelmaking.

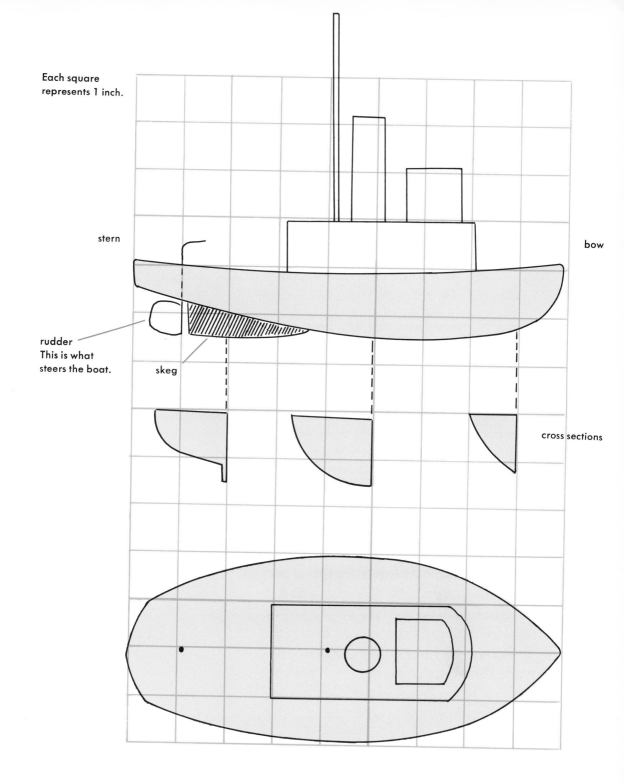

Each square represents 1 inch.

stern

bow

rudder
This is what
steers the boat.

skeg

cross sections

2. Draw the profile or side view of the tug on your block of wood. The shape is quite simple so probably you can trust your eye to get the lines fairly accurately without bothering with the blue squares. Remember the drawings are half size.

3. Now you can start to cut out this "profile shape." It can be done in a variety of ways. Perhaps you know someone with power tools who will do this rough cutting for you. A good rasp will do the job fairly fast, or you can use a hammer and chisel or a pocketknife. You might find that a plane will work best. Make sure that any cutting tools you use are razor-sharp. (See page 7 about how to sharpen tools.)

4. When you have the profile shape roughed out, draw the top view on the top side of the wood. Then proceed to cut away up to these lines, just as you did with the profile. With all cutting, you must be very much aware of how the grain in your wood is running. Always cut in a direction that will produce a neat clean chip, and not long jagged splinters that you can't control. One or two experimental cuts should quickly tell you which is the best direction to work in. Even if you are using a rasp, you should be aware of the grain. The rasp will cut better in some directions than others.

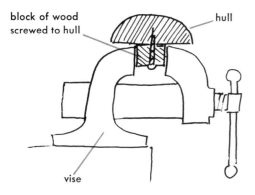

block of wood
screwed to hull

hull

vise

5. After the side and top have been cut out, it would be a good idea to screw a small block of wood temporarily to the deck. The vise can grip this block, enabling you to work more easily on the hull.

6. Now you have something that starts to look a little like a boat, and the fun begins. You can start to round off the hard edges along the bottom, and begin to develop the rounded V shape at the bow. Use whatever tools you find do the job best—knife, chisel, rasp, or an electric drill with a rough sanding disk. Refer to the cross sections frequently. They will tell you just what the curves should look like. But don't feel that you can't make any changes. The plans given here are simply guides. If you feel that you must have a tug with a narrower stern or a bow of a different shape, go ahead and make it that way.

7. When you have the shape of the hull just the way you want it, you can work on the curve of the deck. This is one of the things that makes a tugboat a handsome object. This curve is called the "sheer line." Some boats have a straight sheer line; others—like our tug —have a very curved sheer line. In order to get this curve, you will have to remove the block used to hold the hull in the vise, then do some careful rasping or filing. When you do this, be sure to avoid nicking the edge of the deck. This task

This curve is called
the "sheer line."

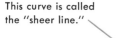

20

is slow and tedious, but if you do the job well, you will greatly improve the looks of your model.

skeg

Carve the skeg from a scrap of wood and attach with glue.

8. The little triangular piece of wood at the stern is called the "skeg." It helps to keep the boat moving through the water in a straight line. The rudder can be made as shown below.

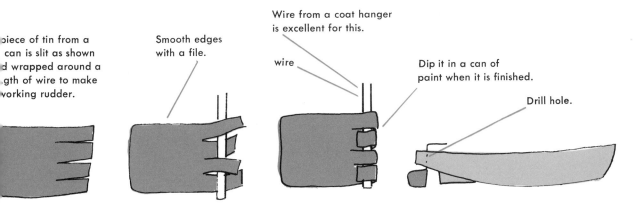

Wire from a coat hanger is excellent for this.

piece of tin from a can is slit as shown d wrapped around a gth of wire to make working rudder.

Smooth edges with a file.

wire

Dip it in a can of paint when it is finished.

Drill hole.

9. When the hull is finished, you've done the most difficult part of the model. The rest is easy. The next two parts you need are the cabin and the wheelhouse. These can be cut from a piece of 2- × 2-inch pine.

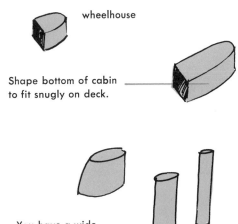

wheelhouse

Shape bottom of cabin to fit snugly on deck.

10. The smokestack can be made from a length of ¾-inch dowel or a piece of broom handle, or you can whittle the shape from a piece of pine 1 inch square. The smokestacks on tugs vary in size. Some of the old-fashioned tugs had tall thin stacks. The more modern and oceangoing tugs usually have squat fat

You have a wide choice of smokestacks.

21

stacks. You'll have to decide for yourself which you prefer. The mast can be a piece of coat-hanger wire or a thin dowel, and it should be set into a hole of the appropriate size drilled in the top of the cabin.

11. If you are going to put your model in the water, you will have to worry about whether the boat is top-heavy or not. If it is, your tug might capsize. Float the hull in a sink full of water with all the superstructure in place. Do not glue anything down yet. If the boat seems tipsy, you will have to reduce the weight of the superstructure. The drawings show a few possible ways of doing this. (You could increase the stability of the hull by adding ballast, such as a piece of lead, to the bottom of the hull. But this would probably make the tug sit too low in the water. Ballast is any weight added to the bottom of a hull for the purpose of making the hull more stable.)

12. The basic model is complete now, and if you want, you can add at this point any little details you think necessary. You might want to add hatches, towing bits, searchlights, railings, radar antenna, and so on. You can buy a propeller for a few cents from a model or hobby shop, and add that. This model is not intended to have a motor, so the

A short smokestack and mast will help to keep your tug from capsizing.

You may have to carve out the insides of the cabin and wheelhouse to save weight.

If you want to add a propeller, it would be placed between the skeg and the rudder.

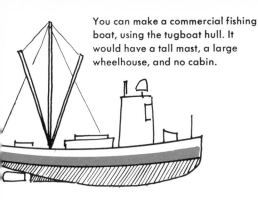

You can make a commercial fishing boat, using the tugboat hull. It would have a tall mast, a large wheelhouse, and no cabin.

A fireboat would have plenty of water nozzles and a big searchlight or two.

nail with point cut off

dowel with a slot

You can make a water nozzle from a piece of dowel and a sawed-off nail.

propeller is only for the sake of appearance. If you want your tugboat to be a fireboat, you can add some of the details shown above. The color scheme for a fireboat would, of course, be bright red with white trim.

13. Before you paint your model, be sure all surfaces are sanded as smooth as possible. Fill all holes (except the hole for the mast!) and nicks with plastic wood or some similar material. You can make your own patching material by mixing with glue the dust from your sanding and filing. Refer to page 10 for information about painting. Don't forget to use masking tape for neat edges. When all the separate parts are painted, you can glue them together. Page 10 has information about gluing.

white stripe (use masking tape)

All sorts of extra details can be added to dress up your tugboat.

Any model looks better if it is supported on a stand. Here are a few possibilities.

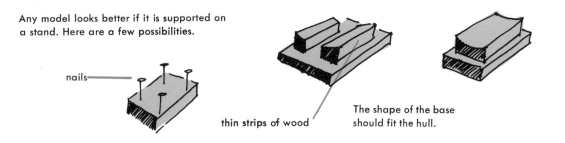

nails

thin strips of wood

The shape of the base should fit the hull.

2. A SIMPLE SAILING MODEL

The model described here has the same type of hull as the tugboat described in the previous chapter. But the cabin, smokestack, etc., are replaced with a mast and sails, and a keel has been added. A model so small won't sail very fast or efficiently. Rough water and strong winds will over-power it. But on a day with gentle breezes and smooth water, it will move right along in a determined fashion. The first time I tried out the model shown in the photo-graph on the opposite page, I took it to a little inlet. I expected it simply to sail across the inlet to the opposite side. But the wind picked up a little and changed direction, and the boat headed straight down the middle of the inlet and into a large river that ran into Long Island Sound. I quickly had to borrow a rowboat and chase after it.

MATERIALS

One piece of 2- × 4-inch wood (or the equivalent), 9 inches long, for the hull

One piece of ⅜-inch dowel, for the mast

One piece of ¼-inch dowel, for the boom and gaff

Thin, stiff metal or plastic for the keel

Two-ounce lead sinker

Cloth for the sail

Five or six feet of heavy thread or fishing line for the rigging

Six small brass screw eyes and other miscellaneous odds and ends

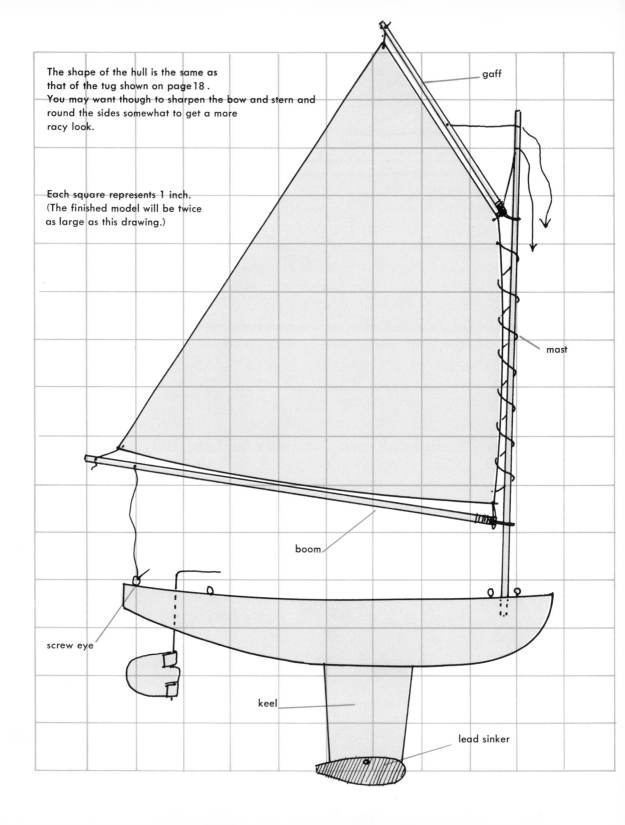

The shape of the hull is the same as
that of the tug shown on page 18.
You may want though to sharpen the bow and stern and
round the sides somewhat to get a more
racy look.

Each square represents 1 inch.
(The finished model will be twice
as large as this drawing.)

gaff

mast

boom

screw eye

keel

lead sinker

1. The directions for making the hull are given in steps 1 through 7 in the preceding chapter. Don't forget that this boat is going into the water, so any glue you use must be the waterproof kind!

2. All sailboats must have a keel. Its purpose is to keep the boat from drifting sideways when the wind is blowing from the side. The keel can be made out of any thin, stiff material such as metal or plastic. The drawings show two different ways of making and attaching the keel.

Smooth edges with a file.

tin

Slit, then bend over.

Drill or punch small holes.

Often the sailing abilities of this model can be greatly improved by shifting the position of the keel. This is one good reason for making the kind of keel that fits into a through-cut slot. With this arrangement it is simple to move the keel forward or backward.

The slot can be made by first drilling a hole in the hull and then sawing with a coping saw or hacksaw blade.

Make sure the keel doesn't drop through the slot. One of the ways to do this is to drill a small hole in the top edge of the keel and fit in a pin.

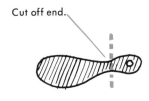

Cut off end.

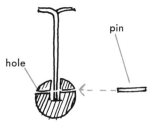

hole

pin

3. Sailboats need ballast as well as a keel. Without it, the wind, blowing against the sail, would knock the boat down. The ballast acts as a counter-weight. The ideal ballast for our little sailboat is a 2-ounce lead sinker which you can get for a few cents in any hardware or sporting goods store. Cut off with a hacksaw the small end of the sinker. Then with the same tool cut a deep groove in it. The keel fits into this groove. The sinker is kept in place by drilling a small hole through both the sinker and the keel. Then a pin is hammered through the hole. This pin can be a sawed-off nail, a piece of heavy copper wire, or whatever you can find that will fit snugly. If you prefer, you can simply drill a hole in the keel and then, with thin copper wire, wrap the sinker to the keel. This wrapping should then be covered with plastic wood, glue, or a filler of some sort to make a neat, streamlined shape.

pin hammered through sinker and keel

hole

The ballast is held in place by string or thin wire.

If you can't get a lead sinker, you could use something like a heavy steel bolt. This will provide the needed weight, but won't be as streamlined or neat as a sinker.

28

A piece of tin from a tin can is slit as shown and wrapped around a length of wire to make a working rudder.

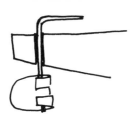

You could also make the rudder from wood. File and sandpaper it to get a streamlined shape.

4. The mast is made of a piece of ⅜-inch dowel. Use a file to taper it slightly at the top. Drill a hole in the deck about an inch deep. It should be the same diameter as the mast so that there will be a snug fit. (Be sure to drill the hole straight!)

5. The boom and the gaff are made from ¼-inch dowels. (The gaff is the short boom that holds up the top edge of the sail.) Drill very small holes in the mast, boom, and gaff, as shown in the plans. The boom and the gaff are fixed to the mast by means of U-shaped pieces of stiff wire, attached as shown in the drawing.

These strings are tied to the screw eyes. (A sailor would call these strings by their proper name: "halyards." A halyard is any rope used for raising or lowering sails.)

a piece of a paper clip

Use thin string or wire to attach U-shaped pieces of stiff wire. Make sure stiff wire is wrapped good and tight. Paint it.

gaff: 10 inches   boom: 13 inches

small holes for attaching sail

6. A piece of old sheet or shirt will do fine for the sail. All edges should be hemmed. Sew on a short piece of string at each corner so that the sail can be attached to the spars.

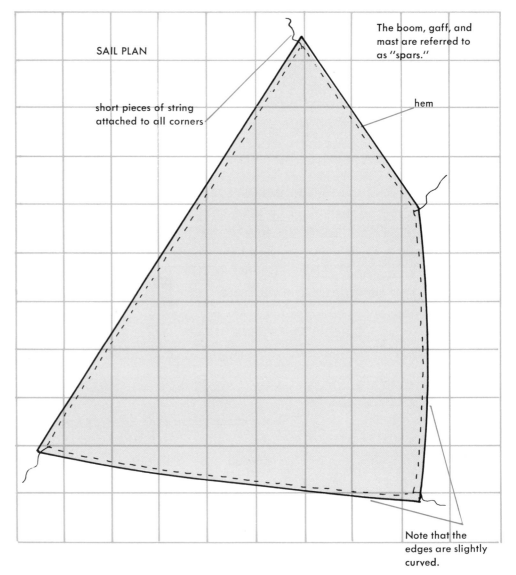

SAIL PLAN

short pieces of string attached to all corners

The boom, gaff, and mast are referred to as "spars."

hem

Note that the edges are slightly curved.

7. There is a thin string called braided squidding line which you can use wherever string is mentioned. This is a very strong nylon fishing line that looks good and works very well on all model boats. You can buy it any place fishing equipment is sold, or if you know someone who fishes, you may be able to get some from him. You only need about five or six feet of it. If you can't find this, use a heavy, strong, white sewing thread.

8. Finally you can paint or varnish both the hull and the spars. The appearance of most models will be greatly improved if you paint a water line on the hull. Use masking tape for a neat job. (Give your boat a name, and paint it on the stern.)

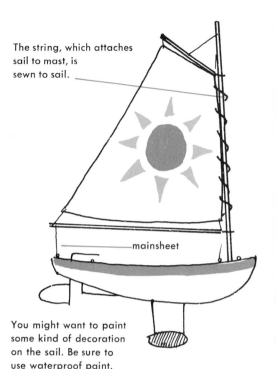

The string, which attaches sail to mast, is sewn to sail.

mainsheet

You might want to paint some kind of decoration on the sail. Be sure to use waterproof paint.

When you sail your boat, you will no doubt have to do a good deal of fiddling and adjusting until you get the boat to perform properly. Adjust the gaff so that there aren't any wrinkles in the sail. Do the same with the string that attaches the sail to the end of the boom. The string that is attached to the end of the boom and goes to the deck is called the mainsheet. It determines how far out the boom will swing. It should not be pulled in very tight. Try it in different positions, and try different positions of the rudder until you find the settings that seem to work best. And don't try to sail on very windy days.

A rubber band is attached to the tiller and screw eyes. This holds the rudder in any position that you want.

3. A MISSISSIPPI RIVER STERN-WHEELER

Riverboats like this were common on the Mississippi River during the nineteenth century. They carried cargo and passengers up and down the river, and were a picturesque sight. The simplified model described here will move along just as gracefully as the original—but instead of cruising the Mississippi, it will only cruise from one end of a bath-tub to the other, or else go for a short distance in the smooth waters of a pond.

The "motor" is a rubber band. The rubber band is stretched across the stern of the boat. A paddle wheel is placed in the loop of the rubber band, which is then twisted up. As the rubber band untwists, the wheel revolves, pushing the boat through the water.

MATERIALS

One piece of pine 1 × 5 inches, 14 inches long, for the hull

Two pieces of thin wood, plastic, or fiberboard about 5 × 8 inches, for the decks

Three feet of lattice wood or balsa wood about ½ inch thick and 1½ inch wide, for cabins and the stern wheel

Short length of ½-inch dowel for the smokestacks

Miscellaneous scraps of wood and odds and ends

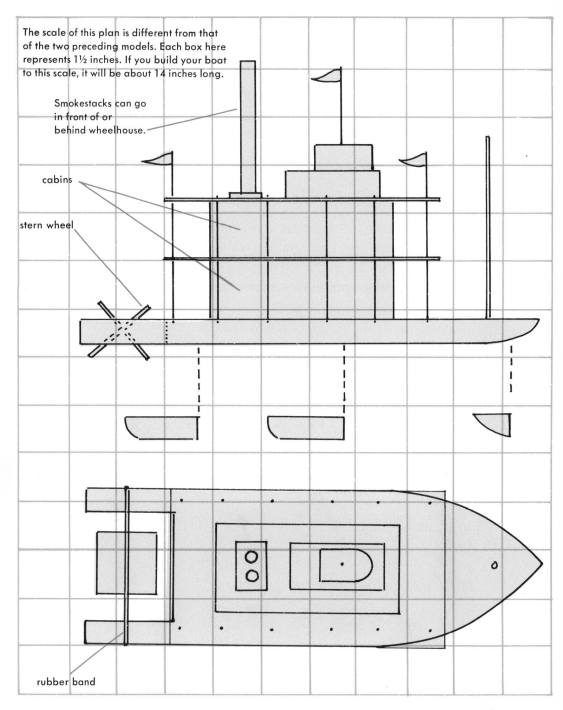

The scale of this plan is different from that of the two preceding models. Each box here represents 1½ inches. If you build your boat to this scale, it will be about 14 inches long.

Smokestacks can go in front of or behind wheelhouse.

cabins

stern wheel

rubber band

34

1. The hull is very simple. All you really have to do is to cut one end of your board into a point for the bow, and then cut a piece out of the stern for the paddle wheel. You can then round off the bottom edges with a plane or file to give the hull a graceful look.

2. The cutout at the stern can be made with a coping saw. If you have any difficulty with this, you can simply make the hull a little shorter than shown on the plans and add two separate strips of wood as in the drawings.

3. If your model is to float without tipping over, you must keep it from being top-heavy. If you make the cabins hollow as shown, using lattice wood, you will be able to save quite a bit of weight. Lattice wood is thin wood stripping about 1½ inches wide and approximately $3/16$ inch thick. For this same reason, balsa wood, which is very light in weight, is a good material for any above-deck structure on this boat.

4. You'll have to find some thin material for the two upper decks. Plywood, balsa wood, plastic, fiberboard (such as Masonite), or any similar material will do. Heavy cardboard might do if you can't find anything else—but it is not a strong nor water-resistant material and is best avoided.

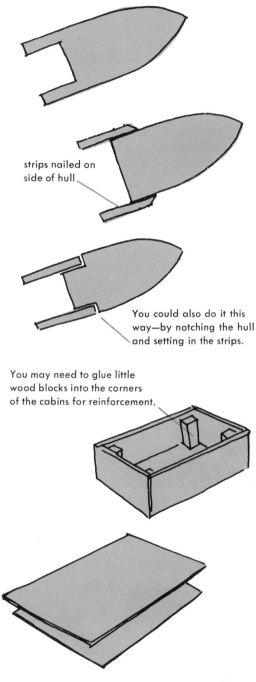

strips nailed on side of hull

You could also do it this way—by notching the hull and setting in the strips.

You may need to glue little wood blocks into the corners of the cabins for reinforcement.

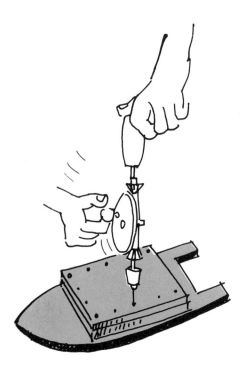

5. The thin columns that support the decks can be made from thin dowels, pieces of coat-hanger wire, or anything similar. When you drill the holes for these columns, it is a good idea to tape or temporarily nail the two decks—one right on top of the other—directly to the hull. Then you can drill through the two decks and into the hull at the same time and be certain that all the holes will line up exactly.

6. The stern wheel is perhaps the trickiest part of this model because it must be light as well as strong. The drawings show several different ways of making it. You can choose the one that best suits the materials available.

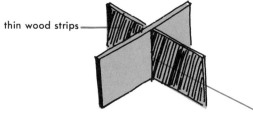

thin wood strips

cement or waterproof glue

You may need to glue thin strips of wood into the corners to strengthen the wheel.

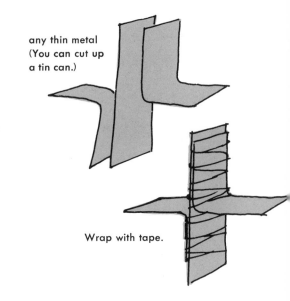

any thin metal
(You can cut up a tin can.)

Wrap with tape.

7. The rubber band that turns the stern wheel should be new and fairly large. (Old rubber bands lose their elasticity.) If you can't find one that seems thick enough, try combining a few, or cut two or three apart and tie the ends together to give you one that is long enough.

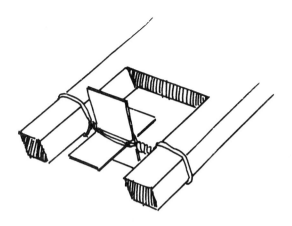

8. Finally you can sand, patch, and assemble all the parts, then paint as described on page 10. These boats were usually all white except for the smokestacks, which were black, and the decks which were gray or brown.

You can turn your stern-wheeler into a night-light by putting a small bulb inside the cabins.

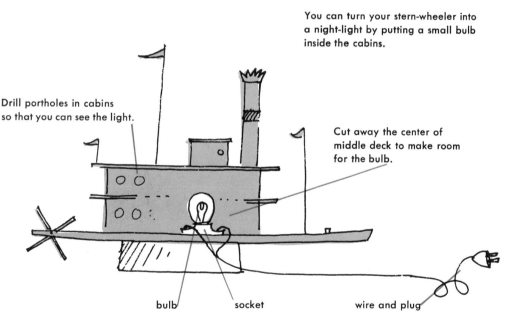

Drill portholes in cabins so that you can see the light.

Cut away the center of middle deck to make room for the bulb.

bulb   socket   wire and plug

Make a stand using scrap wood.

You could also rig up a battery and flashlight bulb.

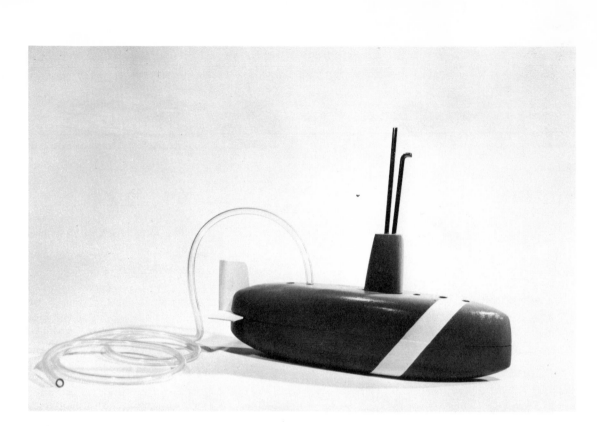

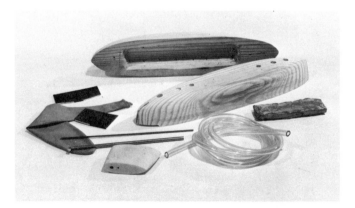

4. SUBMARINES

This submarine can be built in a number of different ways: (1) as a display model; (2) as a working model with a functioning propeller; (3) as a model which has no propeller but which will submerge and rise.

The hull has been designed so that the top and bottom come apart. This will let you place lead ballast and a rubber-band motor inside if you are making a propeller-driven model, or ballast and a rubber balloon inside if you are making a diving model.

If you intend to just keep your model on a stand and not put it in the water, you can carve the hull out of a single block of wood, or two pieces glued together, and not bother with ballast, hollowing out, and many of the other special requirements of a powered or submerging model. In this case you could also modify the plan and make your submarine more sleek and modern-looking.

MATERIALS

Two pieces of 2- $\times$ 3-inch wood, 12 inches long, for the hull

Two pieces of thin metal for the fins (They can be cut out of the lid from a tin can.)

Miscellaneous scraps of wood and odds and ends

Special materials described in the text, depending on which type of model you're making

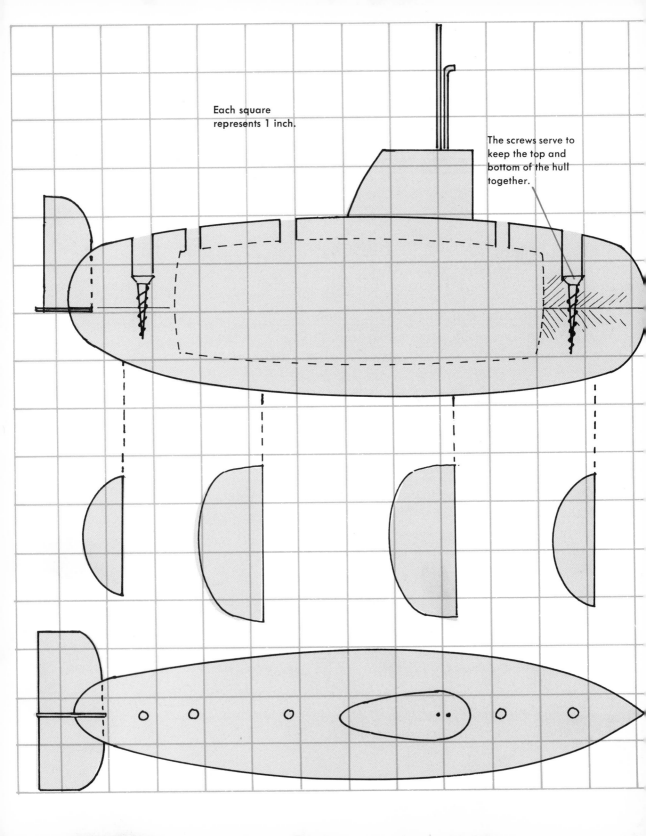

Each square
represents 1 inch.

The screws serve to
keep the top and
bottom of the hull
together.

The following steps show how you can make a submarine that will float or submerge. Then at the end of this section there are some notes and drawings to explain how you can change this submerging model into a working model with a propeller and a rubber-band motor.

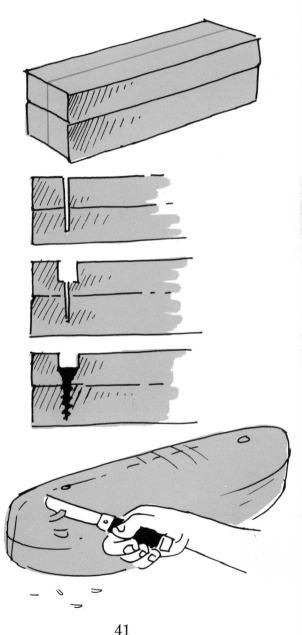

1. Draw a center line along the top, ends, and bottom of the two pieces of wood which will make the hull.

2. Drill a small hole, and then a larger one as shown in the drawings. The small hole is a guide hole for a long screw. The larger hole is so that the head of the same screw can be recessed a good distance below the surface of the wood and not be in the way of your cutting tools when you shape the hull. Drill this "small hole–large hole" combination in both the forward end and aft end of the hull. Then screw the two pieces of wood firmly together. Now you are ready to start shaping.

3. With your chisel, whittling knife, plane, or rasp carve the shape of the hull. The bow should come to a fairly sharp point. The stern should be more blunt—especially if your model is going to have a rubber-band motor and propeller. The shape is not at all critical—just try for graceful, rounded, smooth

41

forms. You can use your own judgment as to what a submarine should look like, or you can closely follow the plans given. You might have some photographs that will give you some ideas. However, you must remember that there has to be room inside the hull for ballast and a balloon.

4. When you have the shape roughed out to your satisfaction, unscrew the two halves and gouge out the insides of both parts. You'll find that the cutting will be easier if you first drill a great many holes in the areas you are going to "excavate." Use a big bit, and be careful not to drill all the way through the hull. Wrap a bit of tape around your bit at the depth you want to cut to. This will be your guide as to how deep to drill. Using a sharp chisel or gouge, you will now be able to finish off the job with a minimum of fuss.

5. Saw two thin slits in the stern— one vertical, one horizontal. Thin metal fins will be cemented into these slits when the model is finished.

6. Make the conning tower from a scrap piece of wood. It can be attached by means of glue and a short length of dowel as shown in the illustration. The periscope is a piece of stiff, heavy wire, bent at the end.

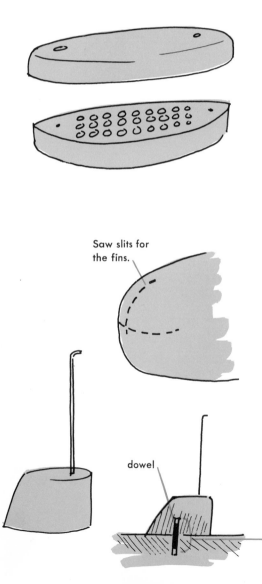

Saw slits for the fins.

dowel

Make sure that the hole in the hull and the hole in the bottom of the conning tower line up. Be sure to use waterproof glue or cement.

7. Unless your model has some ballast it will simply turn on its side and float in a very unsubmarine-like manner. The ballast will make it stay upright, and will also submerge it. The ballast also gives the hull a great deal of weight, so that if you give the model a gentle shove while it is half-submerged it will move for a surprisingly long distance because of its inertia. (The more weight an object has, the more inertia it has, and therefore it will coast along farther when given a push.) The best ballast for this submarine is lead. Several lead fishing sinkers, adding up to about 12 ounces, should do the trick. If you want, you can melt the lead in an old discarded pan and then pour it into the bottom of the hull. (Don't use a pan that someone will cook in because lead is poisonous.) The amount of ballast used is quite important. It should be enough just barely to sink the assembled model. The position of the ballast is also important. Place it so that the weight is centered and the submarine will submerge evenly. You will no doubt have to do a considerable amount of shifting and adding or removing of weight until you get the ballast exactly right. This adjusting is strictly a matter of trial and error.

You'll find that after you have used your submarine awhile, the wood may

Heat the lead just enough to melt it. If it's too hot, you may set the wood on fire.

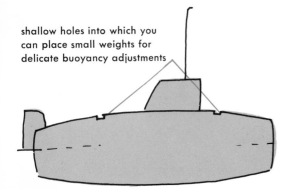

shallow holes into which you can place small weights for delicate buoyancy adjustments

become a little water-logged, and its buoyancy will change. You can make delicate buoyancy adjustments by placing small pieces of lead or screws on the top of the hull. You can drill shallow holes into which these pieces can be placed as needed.

8. In order to raise the submarine from the bottom of the bathtub, or pond, or wherever you will use it, you must increase its buoyancy. This is done by blowing air into a balloon inside the hull. The balloon expands, displacing water (which is inside the hull), and the submarine rises to the surface. The displaced water is forced out of the hull through holes which you must drill through the top of the hull. You can place these holes wherever you like. The best balloon to use is a large, long one.

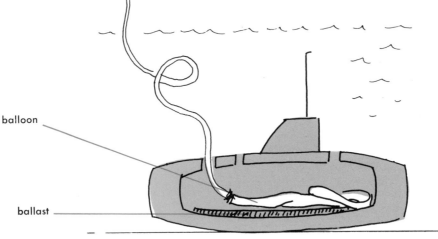

thin hose or tubing

balloon

ballast

The balloon doesn't have to be blown up completely. It has to expand only enough to fill the empty space inside the hull. A small, hard-to-blow-up balloon will not work well. Attach a long, thin plastic or rubber hose to the balloon. If you tightly wrap the balloon with string or wire where it goes over the hose, you should get a leakproof connection. Drill a hole in the top of the hull through which the hose can pass.

9. The hull should be sanded until it is as smooth as possible, then sealed and painted as described on page 10. If you want to paint any stripes, be sure to use masking tape.

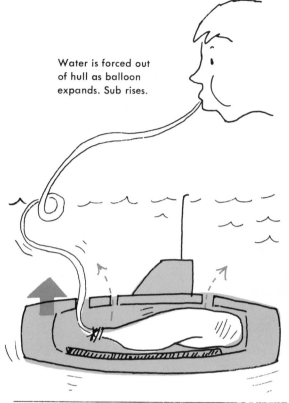

Water is forced out of hull as balloon expands. Sub rises.

A broad stripe across the bow of the sub will improve its appearance.

Instead of a submarine you might prefer to make a diving bell like this. You could use a plastic container either with or without a lid. Use plenty of ballast spread evenly along the bottom edge. You can attach a magnet to the bottom of the bell and go diving for metal objects.

nuts-and-bolts ballast

magnet

Another way to make this submarine is with a rubber-band motor as shown in the drawings here. You can buy a small plastic propeller for a few cents from any model or hobby store. You should also get the shaft that the propeller screws into. If you want, you can quite easily make your own propeller from wood as shown below.

If you remove some ballast and adjust the fins on your submarine, you can get it to start on the surface, then sail downward, and then finally come up to the surface again when the rubber band is unwound and the propeller stops.

This is how you can whittle your own propeller:

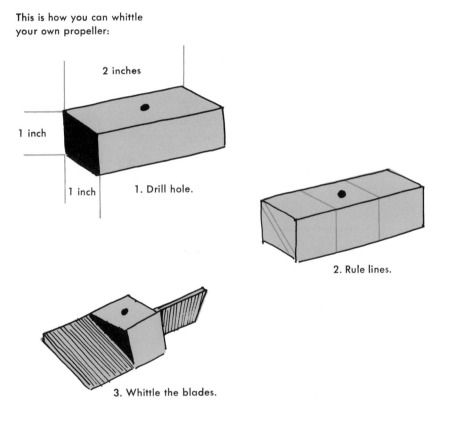

2 inches

1 inch

1 inch   1. Drill hole.

2. Rule lines.

3. Whittle the blades.

A <u>POWERED</u> SUBMARINE

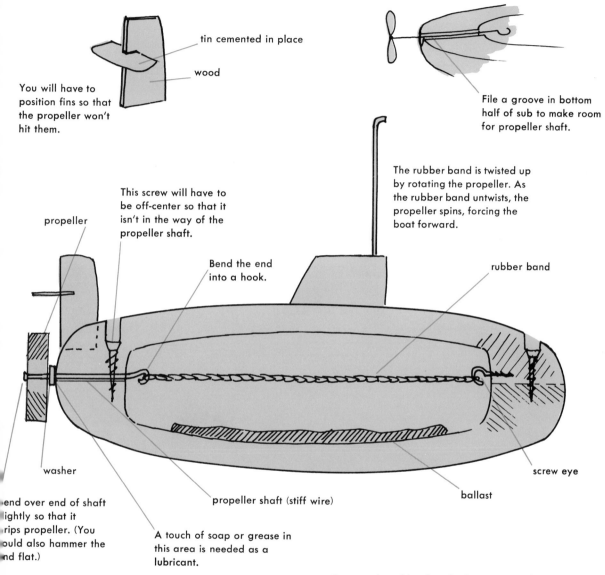

tin cemented in place

wood

You will have to position fins so that the propeller won't hit them.

File a groove in bottom half of sub to make room for propeller shaft.

This screw will have to be off-center so that it isn't in the way of the propeller shaft.

The rubber band is twisted up by rotating the propeller. As the rubber band untwists, the propeller spins, forcing the boat forward.

propeller

Bend the end into a hook.

rubber band

washer

screw eye

end over end of shaft ightly so that it rips propeller. (You ould also hammer the nd flat.)

propeller shaft (stiff wire)

ballast

A touch of soap or grease in this area is needed as a lubricant.

Because the rubber band takes up a good deal of space, it would be difficult to make a powered submarine that would also submerge and rise. The air hose would also interfere with the boat's motion.

5. MAKING A HOLLOW HULL

There are several reasons for making the hull of a model boat hollow. One reason is to make room for various objects inside. If you want a motor in a boat, or if you want a secret compartment to use as a personal hiding place for small valuable objects, you must have a hollow hull. Another reason is that a hollow hull will be much lighter than a solid one, and your model will therefore be more buoyant and easier to propel through the water. This holds true if the means of propulsion is a rubber-band motor, an electric motor, or sails.

There are two ways to hollow out a hull. The simplest is to take the hull when it is roughed out to approximately its final shape, then scoop out the inside with a gouge or chisel. Your tools must be very sharp. Watch the grain of

It is a simple matter to take a sharp chisel and cut away the wood that remains between all these holes. This is a fast and efficient way to hollow out a hull.

48

the wood and cut in a direction that will give you a neat small chip and no splits or long unmanageable splinters. You must work slowly and carefully. You'll get best results when the wood is a good grade of pine, dry and without knotholes. If you drill holes, as described on page 42, the gouging will be much easier.

The other method is to build the hull from several separate layers of wood, with the middle of some of the layers cut out with a coping saw. This is called the "bread-and-butter" method. It is generally used with models

Here are 4 pieces of board shaped, and cut out, and ready to be glued together. The two wood dowels fit through the holes and serve to line up all the layers.

longer than a foot and a half or so. If your hull consisted of five layers, for example, you could cut out the centers of the second, third, and fourth layers. Then, when all five layers are glued together, you will have a hull with a large, empty interior.

This is the procedure for making a bread-and-butter type of hull: (1) Pile your boards (which have been cut to the proper length) one on top of the other. Drill two holes through all five layers. (This same method is used whether you are using three layers or seventeen.) (2) Insert in each hole a snug-fitting dowel that goes through all five layers. This will hold everything together. (3) Now carve the hull. (4) Remove the dowels and cut out the

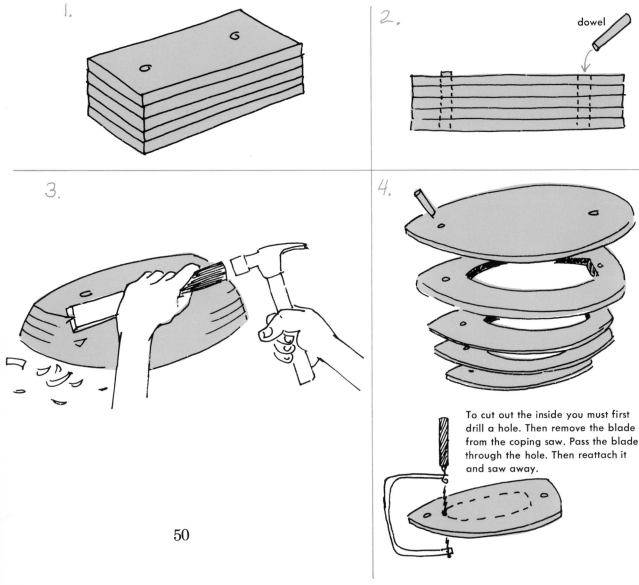

1.

2.

dowel

3.

4.

To cut out the inside you must first drill a hole. Then remove the blade from the coping saw. Pass the blade through the hole. Then reattach it and saw away.

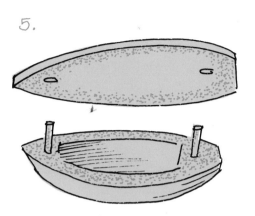

5.

Use plenty of glue.

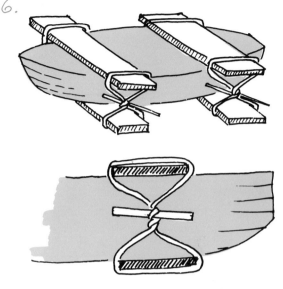

6.

If you don't have any C-clamps you can use boards and rope as shown here. When the rope is twisted up tightly, you get a strong clamping action.

C-clamp

middles of the second, third, and fourth layers. (5) Glue the layers together permanently. Start with the bottom layer and build up. Use the dowels in the two holes as your guides to make sure all the layers line up properly. (6) Clamp the whole thing together until the glue dries. Cut off any projecting ends of the dowels. Then you can use your finishing tools for the final shapes.

6. POWERBOATS

The plans shown here can be used to make a sport fishing boat, a deluxe motor cruiser, a small runabout, or a PT boat. The PT or torpedo boat was powerful and extremely fast, and you have no doubt read about it and seen it in many movies. President Kennedy skippered one in the Pacific. They were designed to be small and fast so that they could get close enough to a large warship to shoot off its torpedoes and then speed safely away.

The hull of a torpedo boat is fairly similar to that of the other types of boats mentioned above. So if you decide you'd rather have one of these you can follow the directions for making the hull and deck of the PT boat, and then make any changes in the superstructure and color scheme to get the kind of boat you want.

MATERIALS

Four pieces of 1- $\times$ 6-inch pine, 18 inches long, for the hull

One piece of thin plywood or fiberboard, 6 $\times$ 18 inches, for the deck

Rubber-band motor or electric motor, etc., described in text, depending on the kind of power you want to use

Miscellaneous scraps of wood and odds and ends

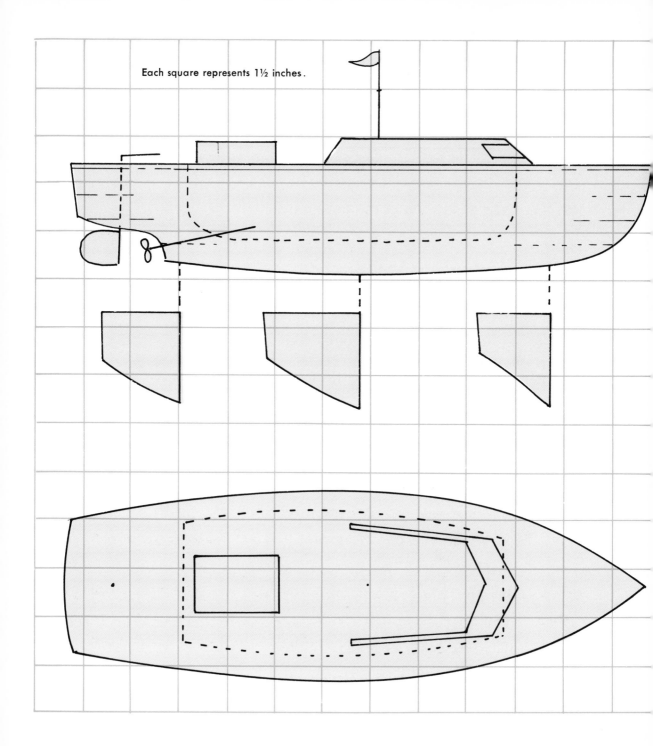

Each square represents 1½ inches.

1. The hollow hull can be made in either of the two ways described in the preceding chapter. Or, if you don't intend to make a working model, you can simply glue the boards together, not bothering with the hollow space or thin deck.

Notice that this hull is quite angular. The sides are flat and almost vertical. The bottom is a wide V shape. The line where the sides and the bottom meet is not rounded but sharp and definite. The underwater portion of the stern of this boat has been cut away to make room for propeller and rudder.

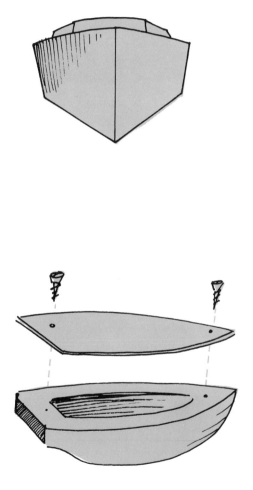

2. After the hull is completed, make the deck. You'll need a thin piece of plywood or fiberboard (such as Masonite) for this. Place the hull upside down on the board, and trace the outline. Then cut out the shape, staying outside the line. This will give you a little extra material which you can file or sand off later to get a perfect fit. The deck can be fastened in place with two screws. It shouldn't be permanently attached because you will have to remove it from time to time to get at the interior to replace batteries or rubber bands or sponge out water that may leak in.

3. What you put on the deck will determine the kind of boat you'll have. The drawings below show some of the possibilities.

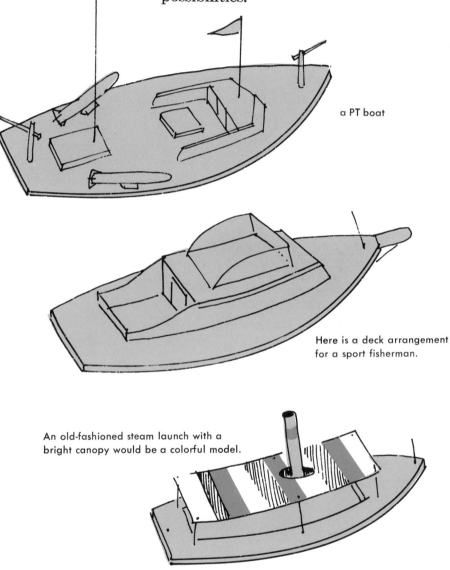

a PT boat

Here is a deck arrangement for a sport fisherman.

An old-fashioned steam launch with a bright canopy would be a colorful model.

4. After the boat is painted, the motor can be put in place. The drawings show how a rubber-band motor is installed. This motor is like the one used to turn the propeller of model airplanes. It is exactly the same as the one used in the submarine, shown on page 47. Be sure to use large, fresh rubber bands. Try to avoid friction where the base of the propeller rubs against the stern. This is a major trouble spot. A little sliver of soap placed at this point can make all the difference between a cranky, sticking action and a smooth, steady motion. You should also make sure that the propeller shaft has no kinks or bends which might bind in the shaft hole.

If you whittle your own propeller, which will be larger than a plastic one, you will have to allow a bigger space for it.

Be sure that propeller shaft doesn't bind. It must be able to turn freely. Fill the hole with vaseline or heavy grease to keep water from leaking into hull.

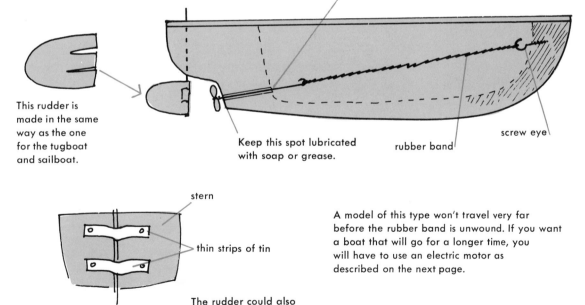

This rudder is made in the same way as the one for the tugboat and sailboat.

Keep this spot lubricated with soap or grease.

rubber band

screw eye

stern

thin strips of tin

The rudder could also be mounted on the stern.

A model of this type won't travel very far before the rubber band is unwound. If you want a boat that will go for a longer time, you will have to use an electric motor as described on the next page.

These drawings show how you can install an electric motor. A hobby or model shop should have a little motor like the one shown, which won't cost much more than a dollar. It should be the kind that works on one 1½-volt D battery. You will also insure best results if you can invest another dollar to get a propeller, propeller shaft, and the little tube into which the shaft will fit. (You can, of course, whittle a propeller and use a piece of stiff, straight wire for the shaft.) The propeller shaft must be attached to the motor in some way. Your model store will probably have a little coupling you can use for this. Or you can look for a piece of rubber or plastic tubing that will fit snugly, without slipping, over both motor shaft and propeller shaft.

When you have all the parts assembled, switch on the motor and adjust its position so that it turns the propeller with the utmost speed and energy. Then glue or nail the motor in this position. It is important that propeller shaft and motor line up perfectly, or else the motor will not be operating at maximum efficiency. Put some heavy grease or Vaseline in the propeller-shaft hole for lubrication and to keep water from leaking into the hull.

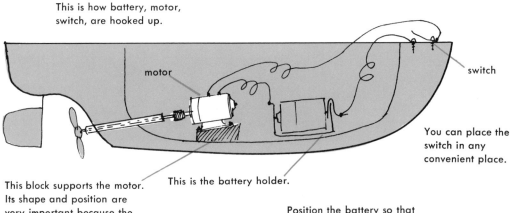

This is how battery, motor, switch, are hooked up.

motor

switch

You can place the switch in any convenient place.

This block supports the motor. Its shape and position are very important because the motor shaft must exactly line up with the propeller shaft.

This is the battery holder.

Position the battery so that the boat is evenly balanced.

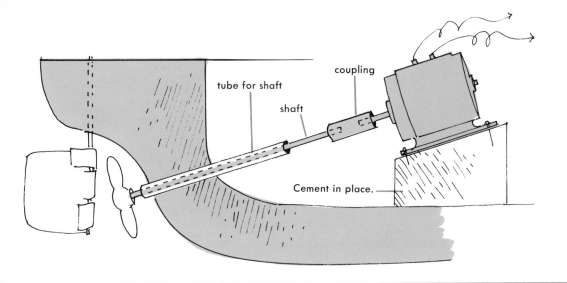

tube for shaft

coupling

shaft

Cement in place.

This is how to make the battery holder:

Cut out and bend pieces of tin as shown. The lid of a tin can will provide the metal.

This fits over the taped end of holder.

This is how the holder looks with the battery in place.

hole

Punch holes with a nail.

hole

hole

holes

battery

Punch in toward where the battery will be, so that the jagged edges of the hole will make a firm contact with the battery terminals. Do this before you bend the tin into shape.

Insulate this part of holder by wrapping with tape. (If you didn't do this, there would be a short circuit with the current coming out of one end of the battery and going directly back in the other end.)

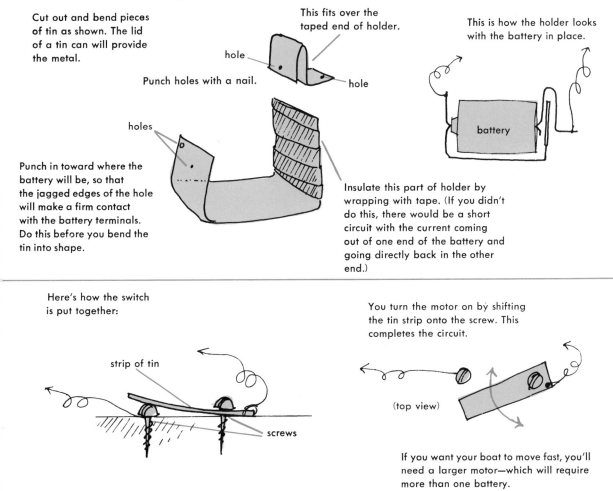

Here's how the switch is put together:

strip of tin

screws

You turn the motor on by shifting the tin strip onto the screw. This completes the circuit.

(top view)

If you want your boat to move fast, you'll need a larger motor—which will require more than one battery.

7. OTHER MODELS

The ship models on the remaining pages of this book are not described in as great detail as the preceding ones. If you've read and tried the construction techniques that have been explained, and made one or two models, you can use the plans given here and change them to suit your own ideas and produce without too much trouble exactly the kind of model you want.

With patience, good materials and tools, and a little ingenuity, you should get good results. I have always enjoyed model boats, partly as works of art and partly as efficient, working, mechanical gadgets. And I am always enormously pleased when they succeed as either one or the other—or sometimes both. I hope you will feel the same way.

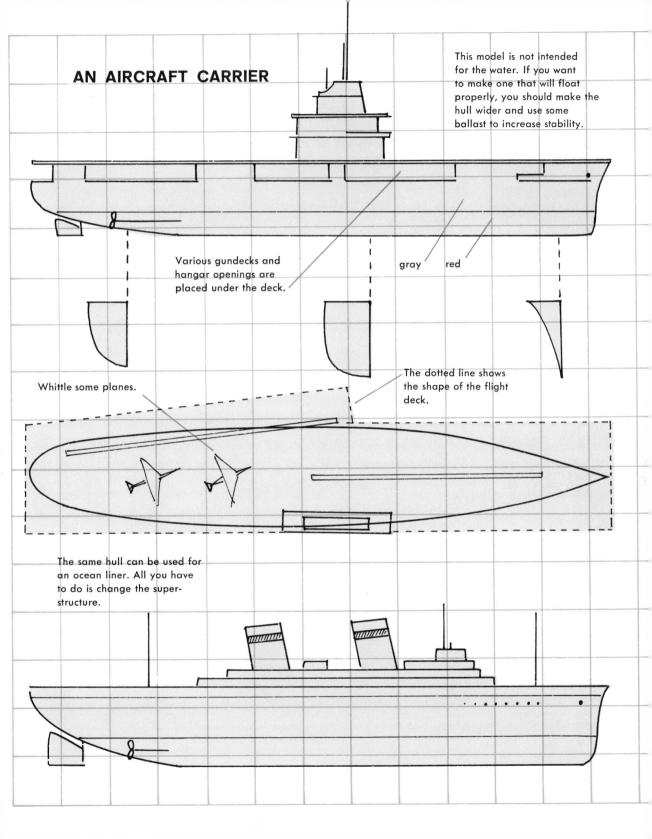

AN AIRCRAFT CARRIER

This model is not intended
for the water. If you want
to make one that will float
properly, you should make the
hull wider and use some
ballast to increase stability.

Various gundecks and
hangar openings are
placed under the deck.

gray   red

The dotted line shows
the shape of the flight
deck.

Whittle some planes.

The same hull can be used for
an ocean liner. All you have
to do is change the superstructure.

The Spray

This is an old-fashioned sailboat based on the design of the vessel that Joshua Slocum sailed single-handed around the world. His book, *Sailing Alone Around the World*, describes his three-year voyage in the *Spray*. It is a fascinating tale, one you should read.

The sails and rigging shown here are similar to those on the small sailboat described in Chapter Two. The *Spray* has an additional sail, however, called a jib. And the entire boat is much larger. The hull should be hollow. Keep it as light as possible. The keel and stem are made of two thin strips of wood attached along the bottom and front edge of the hull. If you are making this model to sail in the water, you will need to attach a considerable amount of ballast to the bottom of the keel to counteract the pressure of the wind on the sails. A bar of lead solder will make fine ballast. If you can't get this, look for any heavy metal weight (about a pound and a half) that can be neatly fitted onto the keel. You may have to shift the position of the ballast until you get the *Spray* sailing most efficiently, so don't attach it permanently until you have a chance to test the boat under sail.

You will also have to experiment with various settings of the sails and rudder until you find just how your boat does under different wind situations. You'll probably find that the boat sails best with the jib trimmed in fairly tight, and the main slacked off somewhat.

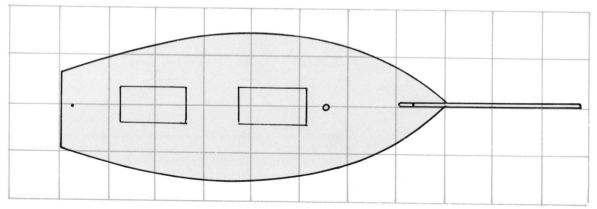

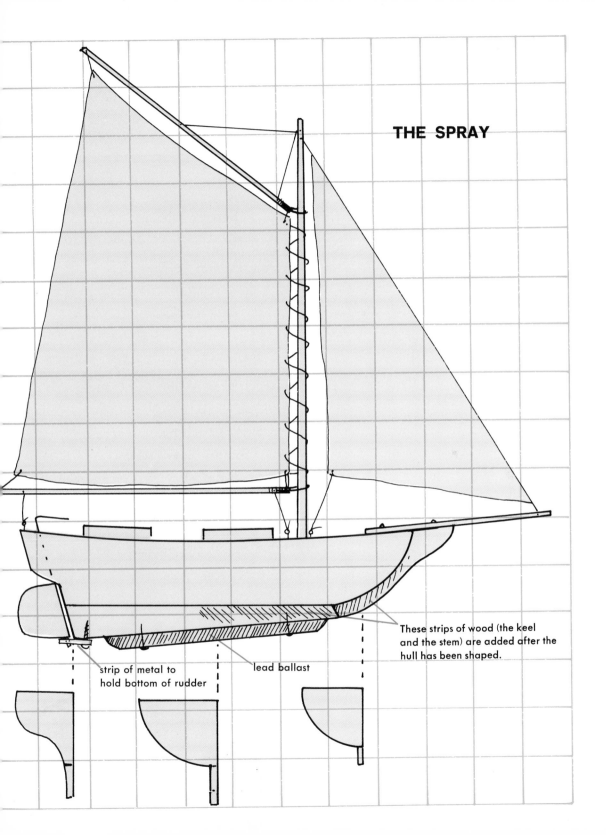

THE SPRAY

These strips of wood (the keel
and the stem) are added after the
hull has been shaped.

strip of metal to
hold bottom of rudder

lead ballast

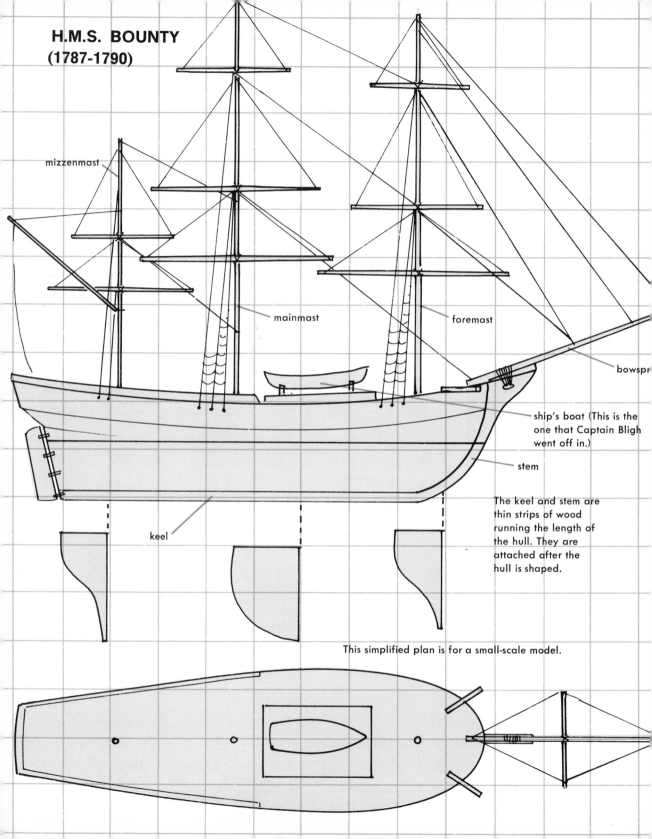

H.M.S. BOUNTY
(1787-1790)

mizzenmast

mainmast

foremast

bowspr

ship's boat (This is the one that Captain Bligh went off in.)

stem

keel

The keel and stem are thin strips of wood running the length of the hull. They are attached after the hull is shaped.

This simplified plan is for a small-scale model.

THE SANTA MARIA (1492)

Nobody knows exactly what Columbus'
flagship looked like. But most experts,
using contemporary drawings and records,
agree that it must have been something
like this.

The area of the sails
is shown by the dotted
lines.

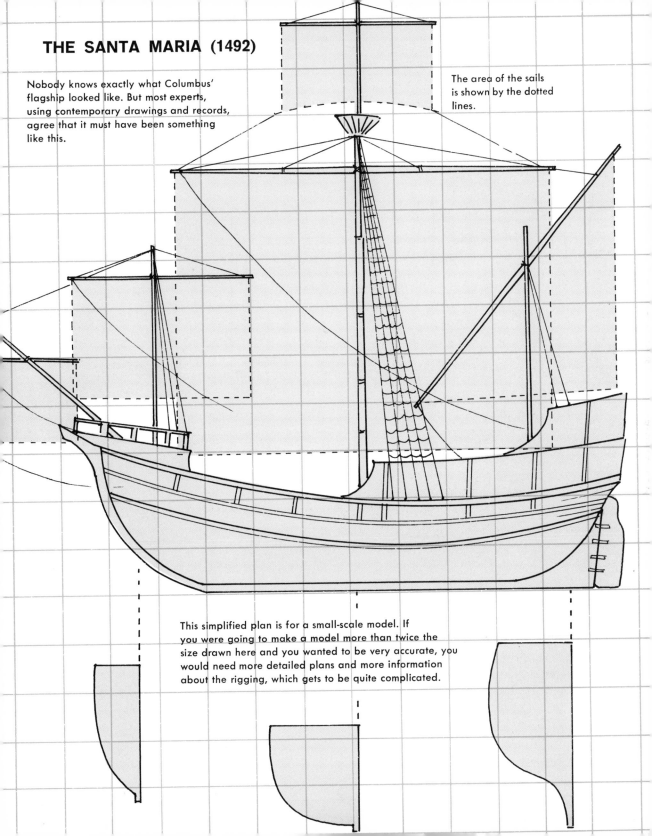

This simplified plan is for a small-scale model. If
you were going to make a model more than twice the
size drawn here and you wanted to be very accurate, you
would need more detailed plans and more information
about the rigging, which gets to be quite complicated.

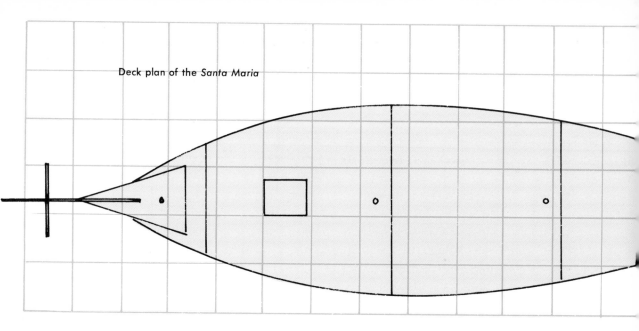

Deck plan of the *Santa Maria*

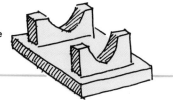

This kind of model is for display. Make a stand for it.

About the Author – Illustrator

Harvey Weiss is a sculptor, whose work is in many museums and private collections. He has done a number of other things, from photography to teaching, but finds writing and illustrating children's books the most stimulating and satisfying.

Mr. Weiss, who lives in Connecticut, is an inveterate builder of ship models. "I have always enjoyed model boats, partly as works of art and partly as efficient, working, mechanical gadgets," he writes. "And I am always enormously pleased when they succeed as either one or the other—or sometimes both. I am particularly proud of a recently finished large-scale model of a tugboat that has a working steam engine, complete with boiler, valves, pumps, gauges, and a very shrill steam whistle. The model is over three feet long, and so heavy I can barely lift it. I am embarrassed to admit the amount of time, money, and effort that I have spent on this one model—but whenever I look at it or use it, I have such an enormous good time that I have absolutely no regrets."